finding june

emily zeigler

for every human being who has lost hope

week 1: relapse

tremors

our bodies are always
shaking.
our veins are always
pumping.
the blood is always
flowing -

the tremors are signals of life.

so during those moments
when my body's quaking
and my eyes darting,
and quick tears snake down my face -
when my lungs threaten
to expand and collapse,
and my bones shake off my skin -

maybe then, i am most alive.

my life began in the after june --
i woke up with the sun.
white rays poked out
through tender clouds,
extending across the horizon.

i doodled circles around the singing tree
when the annual blossoms bloomed.
the singing tree, she swallowed me,
weaving me a loving cocoon.

one year flew by when finally i
awoke to the singing tree's sweet swoons.
but the same sun, he beckoned me
catching me in his playful tune.

sometimes when i pass over her woods,
i return to the singing tree ---
aware of her fraying roots,
so wistful in her recluse....

my sun burned bright with love for me,
calling me closer to his embrace.
i looked down one last time to see
my woods, aflame.

i could barely think think think

i banged on the walls
(covered and covered in art art art)
pretty things faded away
(me me me)

i crashed into the mirror
(blood trickling down down down)
i pressed a cloth to my skin
and stared as my reflection
refused to say thanks thanks

he asks me whenever whenever
"why can't you see your beauty"
so i gaze at him
before i walk away and away
until i tumble down
and echo the screams within me me me

i destroyed my skin
(dried blood under under my nails)
he burst into the room
and grabbed my body in his arms
and cried with me me me

"your scars won't fade"
they solemnly told me -
i smiled for the first time
grateful for this opportunity
for my mind
not to fade away from me.

the colors do not match ---
    they do not mix ---
the colors burst from inside of me.
    red comes first,
through thin lines, crisscrossing my body.
i am the color of the sky.

june was a dream –
     sometimes i
         forget.

he was *my* june dream,
     a summer godsend –
soothing, intoxicating,
awakening my senses.

he kissed me like it was july –
tender touches under a scorching sun.
he had soft healing hands,
mending where i was undone.

he became an august apparition,
entrancing me with his beauty –
but as i continued to reach,
he slowly faded from me.

he shivered at our septembral love:
     the two blankets and empty space.
he had promised to stay til october,
     to drive away the ghosts in november,
         but it was no longer his place.

he had whispered fake promises of a december,
where he'd shelter me in brittle air
and make me laugh by the fire
of a passion we once shared.

he was no longer my january sanctuary,
and june was a dream
of a heat that was never there.

i spin and spin and spin –
i am the earth.
he is the sun, holding me close,
with his gravity.

he lulls me back and forth
as i circle and circle -
i am the revolver
until he takes fire.

he keeps me stable, centered,
moving and alive -
but the strength of his light
is drawn from more than one source.

his other lovers and i
twirl around him -
we are the prettiest colors in the galaxy.
yet no matter how close
he tugs our heavenly bodies
towards him,
we know that a true collision
would only collapse our balanced
orbits.

only sometimes

sometimes, his laugh was gentler than his touch
and other times, his laugh spread faster than the flu;
like a virus, it contaminated me.

sometimes, his voice was silkier than the moon.

his eyes were the color of scorched hopes and dreams –
sometimes, his aura touched me where his hands would not,
sending shudders through my bones and
frantic messages to my fingertips.

sometimes, he destroyed me -
and passion became the past and
desire was devastation.

you are the moon
and i am the sea −
despite my yearning tides,
you recoil beyond my reach.

you know i can't touch you,
yet you still tease.
stripping - you're stripping −
me of my sanity,
oh, just one caress i need.

your figure dismantles my reason,
your reflection dances through me.
darling, you torment my soul,
as you twirl beyond my boundaries.

why continue
to disregard
my craving waves?
why must i
wait
covetingly
,until you're called
to another constellation?

trigger

the war lives on – burning and screaming –
who is me?
i sit in classrooms:
grasping for a clamp
to anchor me
to that reality.

bullets were confetti
and it was my birthday party.
i hailed the sky
and cowered to my knees, my stomach,
and prayed and shook —

now they stare at me,
my teammates are classmates
but they are no friends of mine.
my hands are empty:
i hold no control.

i gasp, my lungs beg for a draft —of air, of air —
but my body submits to a draft of war
and i submit to the triggers and the trauma and the
worst of me.

apoptosis

i began life as a cell
,cradled in my mother's womb
(i grew and grew, much more, i grew)
one day, i followed design
and she cradled me again, a second time.

she knew me – her child,
her one and only me

each soul, a purpose,
a routine, a role:
we are programmed
to be predictable and

under His control —

when i was in her womb,

my fingers and toes were webbed –
but skin separated, and
cells died instead

the signals from my
chemical brain
run down my skin.
i shrink, i distress,
then i am no more
than a cell again.

after all, He created
many more cells than He needed.
(even though my mother only had
one of me)

week 2: ruin

some people proclaim to be born again,
to be alive, anew, alight.
yet through the same
life-changing circumstances:
i know you can die twice.

death will never simply be when your heart stops
beating
,your brain sends last signals,
or when you lose consciousness forever.
if you are lucky, this
is the only death you will receive.

if you are lucky, you will die once.
it will be instantaneous.
it will be glorious.

(most people die twice)

my brother lost his life when
he lost its importance.
(maybe he was too old,
too sick,
too sad)
he finally understood his true character:
this realization killed all his
hopes, opportunities, dreams --- and
part of him too.
he killed the rest of himself.

when he did not care,
he was truly gone.

when i was three

when i was three, i was convinced that i was the
luckiest.
oh, my father, he could pick up the world
with his own two hands.

my mother was the kindest – she could calm a storm
like me.
and i loved my brothers
like family.

my best friend was my best friend, and
my enemies were my best friends too.
i giggled at my fears and laughed at the dark.

(when i was three, i didn't inherit my mother's common
sense.
oh, my father, he slammed me to the ground and i
couldn't breathe.
one night, my mother's friend stayed over – he
acquainted me with her belt.
and i begged, i begged, my brothers to please let me out.

my teddy bear was there when i slept in the closet,
while i heard voices through the door.
i clasped my hands together
and kissed goodnight to my blisters.)

i still kiss my scars goodnight.

the rope

1. rope twisted around her limbs,
as tightly knotted hair –
at first, he asked her to sing,
(so she screamed until)
beating her, so she murmured her favorite lullaby.
only two weeks of being captivated by her
(he knew he loved her)
, and today was the first day he would make her
his own
(she screamed.)

2. rope tied her hands together –
she begged, she begged,
("please tie them in front")
and she prayed, she prayed,
shifting to her knees
and searching for heaven
in the low, wooden ceiling

3. rope digging into her wrists
while she struggles in vain.
smiling when he glanced at her
(teeth grit in pain)
,but his glazed eyes began to stare more at her
than his eighth bottle of beer.
"don't you love me?" he rasped,
turning the near empty glass in his hands.
(she held her breath)
"WHY DON'T YOU LOVE ME?" as the glass
cracked and
he attacked.

4. rope was comforting if she
dreamt it was a friendship bracelet,
connecting her to her sister, her family.
(yes, the red lines caused by the friction
and tautness of the rope
hurt nicer

than the red lines on her face) –
he straddled her
and traced
and carved

with hands of steel and shards of glass –
she thought of family
and wondered how
such a wicked man entered in.

5. rope lay on the floor beside her,

as she peacefully slept –
he was not supposed to love her, he wept,
as he knew his love failed.
so he took it upon himself to

destroy all the evidence –
her screams were thicker than the fumes,
her red-traced body morphed to black,
and as she burned to death, she
hoped, she wished that he would
burn, burn, *burn* after death.

i would call you out by name ,but
when did you ever recognize my voice?

i was confident in my love,
you in your abilities:
body in yours, tongue's twisted,

hands bound — so *sure*
it was love.

you gave me one option
and i made my choice —
it was freedom,
it was lust,
i was a prisoner
to your touch.

now — where is your heat?
i cannot shout loud enough
to reach you across the empty sheets.
"i love you, i love you!
i will stay, i will stay!"

it was my choice to stay.
it was your choice to release me.

(i created the biggest storm -
i drowned in my own sea)
he drowned in concern
and soothed the shaking out of me

(my skin is a pattern of waves and tides
and my mind is only a torn memory)
i marked him where he was mine
but demanded he set me free

(i threw myself and gladly choked
on the overflowing deadly hopes and dreams)
he swore me out of silence
and taught me to release my screams

(my body could never make it to the bottom of the sea
when i'd wake i'd find it lying on the beach)
a piece of me died when i let his comforting words in,
but my existence collapsed when he finally left.

(my eyes are the curtains to my bedroom windows.
my kisses are nails in the wall.)

i kiss him in the winter
(pin. him. down.)
destroying more than i want -
so i slept
sobbed
surrendered
my lover -
until i faded away.

(the future is fleeting. bury it behind.)

ten months, i am healed,
i am an infant again.
i have tender feet and a big airhead.

my eyes are blue and my mouth is wide.
he feeds on me and me his pride.

my body is a crossweb of silhouettes.
i am connected and controlled by strings
(spiders ate my eyes because,
i see i do i feel i die)
my bed is thorns and my pillows are bones
my pillows are thorns and i am bones.

sanity

"you don't know me"
i broke my own walls
i tore down my self-esteem

"you thought you could help"
i lashed out at myself
i cursed my own name - - -

"you wanted to be the best part of me"
i loathed my skin
my body was
a wasteland.

"you"
i let my sanity go.

you died a thousand times before letting me save you —
did you really hate the face that you gave me?

your skin was a cracked desert where
you managed to conceal your secrets
your teeth were a perfect set of white
but your bark was worse than your bite.

you couldn't break the reflection of you —
but *i* am not your reflection
i am more than your child

still you complain every day of aches and joints that
creak
you scream every night, then proclaim that you are
meek
you laughed and told them that *i* was trouble,
that you'll be sure, you'll be sure, to train me well.

i needed to love you; i needed your comfort —
but how could i love the creator who made me suffer?

i wave white flags to death
calling "please find me, please comfort me"

no, death does not call back
black stains -

i venture out to the streets
and buy
white paint

i color my brown skin
and black black hair
mix in my tears and
dip my bitten nails

plaster covers my face and
i lost my voice ages ago, so
those who only see
a flailing ghost
run.

"i found you, do you need help?"

asks the world, seeing only blood-colored eyes
and red flags.

your touch was a warm flame but it was nothing gentle
as you struggled to keep our love boiling
when you placed your arms around me.
i placed my head to your chest and listened to the
echoes
of blood spurting out
with nowhere to go.

your laugh chimed like bells but they were death's toll,
as your clanging voice boomed in the room,
every one of your strikes reverberated through me.
i fell to the ground and screamed my pleas
but you never heard me.
you never did.

'gift from god' said my mother, holding me —
growing, i gain love, dreams, and
sadness too.
'jane,' she says, 'people who kill themselves go to hell'

less

my company sans compathy
mocks me,

my (melancholic alcoholic) self,
is,
drunk on expectations,
drunk above social outcastes —

methamphetamine, where is your cure?
cure my curse — cure
me of misery.

gods above, are you there?
magnificent, wonderful gods,
i beg, i beg, muster some love for me
provide comfort and shelter
and something for me.

i am mourning, preparing,
a coffin,
for my funeral.
i maneuver my body,
cover me up,
until i am a mound,
a mound of dust.

he glanced at me in the deepest blue —
(i was the smallest fish in the sea)
whispered i was perfect, smirking,
claiming that brown suited me

his arms were the kindest pet pythons
(the only ones i've ever met):
they were secure but i knew if i glanced away,
i knew they'd bring me death

he memorized the inner linings of my soul
(he took my breath away)
the sting of his probing fingers shocked me,
but i didn't dare be afraid

he loved me more than i loved the sky
(but soon enough i only loved him)
and some days i swear, i see his figure
just when the light seems to dim.

i loved you despite

you clawed your hair out, and
your legs were as red
as your dark brown eyes.
you were your own design
and i could not change you -
i loved you despite.

every morning, you lied on the ground —
you lied to me too.
every night, you screamed —
and i stayed to watch, as
sobs dislocated your soul.

you kept knives in your drawer,
but i knew you'd never harm me —
except for when
your scars were fresh.
i loved you despite.

your flesh was marred —
it was beautiful. i kiss it.
your face is struck with shadows.
you were beautiful. i kiss you.
i loved you despite.

i wade through my home,
nearly suffocating.
my feet — black, calloused, bleeding —
are pricked by leftover tacks
(accidents we ignored).

broken dinner plates
and walls,
— adorned with holes and
brown streaks —
are familiar welcomes
as i press against the table,
squeezing past stacks of recycling
we never gave away.

mama cooks in the kitchen —
she reuses pots and pans
and warms up the same old dirt
that we couldn't eat yesterday.

i bend under the hanging wires
and shove past the cleaner clothes,
cracking open the door to my sanctuary
(welcoming me with more shadows).

if i could burn one last time, i'd set you aflame

all my friends tell me about how the loves of their lives
shine like the sun for them;
but when i met my love, he was an electronic lighter
and i was an old candle.

for every time we touched, my blood sparked and fire
spread through my veins.
every time we talked, i wore scarlet on my skin and
clingy clothes with sweat stains.
every time we dared to meet, i knew
it was just one more rendezvous
closer to when i'd lose him and go insane.
i loved him oh-so-much and couldn't afford to never see
him again.

so i burned and burned and BURNED for him —
risked setting the world on fire
as i unguarded my flames and defended my love.
as the strands of passion that tethered us together
became enflamed candle wicks,
he screamed and demanded to know why i was
burning him (and part of me too)

and when he left me,
i was a deserted puddle of wax
and he went to light up another girl's life.

i compete with my past to beat my future.
i am jealous of me, of my capabilities.
together, we win.
together, we destroy —
all future possibilities.

i live my own life

i wrote my name repetitively
holding on to the last fact
that your lies did not corrupt,
i lost track of who i was
and who i will be
but you did not break me.

i punched the closet mirror
and adored my shattered reflection —
i fix my problems with the superglue you left
after you took everything i had
but you did not break me.

never again will i entreat you to
my faults.
you cannot lift
the burdens
that i *gently* hold
as they crush me.

you did not break me.
i broke myself.

week 3: recovery

the day i gave up was the day i was redeemed —
the less i knew i deserved,
the more grateful i was to receive.
so i forgave my mother and
clung to her like the babe i was, and
she took me back into her patient arms.

the day i cried was when the tears dried —
i chose to let go of my control
and quickly sought peace.

the day my heart melted was the day my love
strengthened -
my walls broke down but the stairs were building up
and now i touch my sky with my own hands.

i turn to the earth, and i finally know -
i'm going home,
no matter which direction i go.

i am frayed,
split down my center.
— *snap* —
i break again.
mourn me, pity me,
watch me as
i grow from my roots again.

i ran away at age eight
and found myself in Hell.
i enjoyed the suffering
that i deserved
and *chose* to stay as well.

one year, one month, one day —
my Father called me home.
i trembled at His mercy
and cried at His loving tone.

my Father had called me by my name
every single hour.
it wasn't til i humbled down
that i could finally be found.

i let go of june
and breathed
in honey
for the first time.

i looked into the mirror
and chose to love
the sugar brown skin
and the hurting soul within.

i bled out the evil spirits
and stitched myself clean
i scrubbed away my sins
until my skin gleamed.

i inspected my (new) body
and resolved
to never stop loving me again.

therapy

"talk to me"
you open your mouth
like a fish
but you are drowning
she taps the pen against the clipboard
tap, tap, tap
you are trapped in a tank,
unable to breathe.

"talk to me"
you start with a word or two,
and like a mother with a babe,
she patiently unwinds you –
picks you apart
and understands you.

"talk to me"
the best part of your week:
when you get to blabber
and bemoan your life.
she listens, like
an empathetic reflection,
and you watch as
the dark blue circles fade
and you're capable of
smiling again.

"talk to me"
you comply,
but now,
you can do so much more.
you formed connections,
built yourself up,
and you've strengthened your core.
you are not drowning,
you are not gone –
you saved yourself.

the gentle flakes of snow land on the skin
your hands once touched.
the three wool blankets are not
nearly enough to keep me warm.
my mug of hot cocoa
is not as sweet as your kisses.

but i no longer rely on your heat:
i must endure the cold on my own —

until the summer comes,
i am strong enough
to not freeze away.

he found his joy
in the strangest ways:

the curl of her lips
and the fine laughter lines.
the length of her fingers
with his intertwined.

the flow of her hair
as the he swept her away.
the way her eyes twinkled,
as she whispered,
"you are mine"

they found their joy
together.

(it takes time)

do not punish yourself for not being perfect;
the Maker has sketched you before time began,
and He will continue to mold you into a masterpiece.

my stay in july

i hated the moon but he showed me the stars;
in return i revealed every delicate scar.
i hated the night until he became my light
and for once, for once, i wished i could fight.

if i were alive, if i could survive,
maybe, just maybe, i could stay by his side.
if he doesn't go, if he could just know
how much i'd love to stay in july.

and when he forgets, i will never regret
all of the love and kisses and how i'm indebted.
when our love fades - if our love fades -
i promise i'll never be too far away.

healing takes two and three

mommy made me breakfast
just two days ago
her knees were groaning
but she was smiling
just like two years ago.

daddy set down the paper
to kiss me good morning.
he glanced up at mommy
and was smiling
just like two years ago.

wildflower

dusty roots gnawing at the stone,
firmly setting in.

piercing from the crooked shadows
she yawns in the sun –
warmth tingling through her stem.

her sisters sprouted near her
and ants were in her hair.
she may not live for very long,
but this peace, this bliss, was worthwhile.

remedy recipe

pour two cups of power,
one overflowing cup of joy,
and three tablespoons of gratitude
into your crimson-clay bowl of hope.
sprinkle some laughter for the fluffiness,
and stir until creamy thick.

mix in one cup of chopped courage,
and an ounce or two of golden strength.
pour into your heart-
shaped pan,
and bake until golden brown and sweet.
once cooled, spread on a thick layer of acceptance.
eat whenever ready.
(serves an infinite amount of people)

you are a firefly.

you illuminate the room
and attract others with your light.
enclosed in your jar,
you're a treasure during the day,
but even lovelier at night.

but do not be afraid
to escape the vessel
and fly out to the glade.
your prison may be beautiful
but it is not worth
your entire soul.

i lied crumpled in the arena —
until an unexpected aria arrived
and i listened, struck in grief,
to her comforting melody.

when you feel like this, that means it is time
to pick yourself up
and keep moving on.

"but," i beg,
"what if i always feel like this?"

that means you are a warrior.

fallen, sobbing,
surrounded by bathroom graffiti
and soothing spirits,
i have never felt stronger

let me tell you how Poetry is made:
Poetry is.

week 4: resilience

strength is not always:
mighty bursts of power,
exuberant greatness,
fervent passion.

strength can be found
in the midst of peace;
it is quiet perseverance,
respectful love,
and gentle honesty.

it is in the knots of your hair
after a good night's sleep,
and in the bowl of cereal
you manage to eat.

it is looking in the mirror
and refraining from insults.
it is crying when you need to,
then getting up after.

strength is found
in every action that you do.
darling, you
are the strongest i've ever met.

i will not be a Barbie daughter:
wealthy enough to afford steel
but sure as hell
unable to weld it.

you are more than a puddle of tears;

do not let others walk over you.

do not let unworthy dogs drink from you,

lest they die from the salt.

you cannot hold me back anymore.
i will soar through the galaxies
on my own.
i will no longer depend on you
for survival. my heart was made
for me, my soul was made for me,
my body was made for me --
i do not need to share
my cosmic glory with you.

willpower

a thought is as fleeting as a cloud,
catching you and
sweeping you
to highs you've never known.

a thought is as fleeting as sugar
sweet and lovely on the tongue
until you swallow and the sugar festers
and slowly rots you from inside out.

do not allow dirtiness
disguise itself as pleasure.
do not tempt yourself
and dive into sin.

she was the meadow; the meadow was she.
her eyelids fluttered and her flowers yawned.
the perennials were trapped in serendipity
and so were the rivers, squirrels, and fawn.
the sun poured love all over his meadow ---
and she was alive, alive, alive!

burn in heaven

love pours in and overflows -
it tingles through her blood and drips
(from her delicate fingertips)

tracing, the shape of his face, she
leans in and her lips
are the color of love.

he feels tingles in his spine
and drowns in the heat.
if this is
how he dies
then he will gladly burn in heaven
daily.

i refuse to be "too much"

when i was three, i saw my mama
step onto a scale and sigh disappointedly.
she pointed to an old photo,
"i used to be skinny"

when i was five, my aunt told me
that some women don't wear bikinis anymore
because of their striped and streaked scars.
my mama got those marks
because she had me.

when i was eight, i couldn't help but laugh
as i hopped on and off the scale -
until the number became more and more
significant.
and i remember when the number
became too much.
i was too much fat
and not good enough.

since then, i have grown.
i have recovered.
i am strong, and
i refuse to spend fifteen more years of my life
lamenting over a three digit number,

"the sky is red"
your parents may tell you.
"the sky is red"
if you never dare
to open your window.

if the sky is red (to you),
then you will never see the sky
bluer than water,
pinker than coral,
as bright as innocence
and deeper than your soul.

burst every window and door,
watch the shifting colors,
and breathe the same wind that travels with the clouds.

the Creator wants you to transcend beyond.
He has gifted you, blessed you,
shown you the path to exaltation.

He has provided your iron rod
to guide you through the mists of darkness.

do not fear taking the first step.

hell is cotton-white —
a blank page
of good
that men never chose to do.

i salvaged the specks of light
from the supernova of my sun -
i spread the shreds of my heart
and shared with his devastated lovers.

i will not be selfish
and stash all the mementos
of a man who never belonged to me.
and i swear,
from my fiery melting core
to the foundations of my being,
i will move on
from the man who never belonged to me.

to live, not exist

courage was
waking to a world that refused
to mutter my name
strength was
bursting forth from
the furies of hell that were my cage

[determination]
when i decided that i wanted to
L I V E;
threw away the destiny that remained negative
[success]
when i chose to act instead of
W I S H;
built up the energy when desiring more than just exist

(when i existed, i was a child who couldn't scream
when pitch black took her in the night
i fell from a beautiful blue sky
when i chose my own flight
my butterfly wings
morphed into barricades of iron
and i was never alive
because i was anchored tightly down)

but when i lived i did what i ought
so i could atone,
i SHOUTED into the dusk
until i found my way home...
i broke my steel bonds
and took my mother's hand
and when i lived i could figure out
just where i could stand

and when i created that world that admired my name,
i rose up from the ashes and adored my own fame.

author's note

finding june is a collection of poems written in 2014-18. these poems were written during tough trials in my life. others were written after i sought help.

most of the poems in *finding june* describe events that are fictional. for some, you may feel as though these poems represent your feelings and experiences.

seeking help can seem difficult, but trust me, it is worth it. your family loves you, your friends love you, God loves you, and so do many others. if you are struggling with mental health or any other issues in your life, please talk to a school counselor, your doctor, or a trusted friend that can help you find good resources.

(US national suicide hotline: 1-800-273-8255)

acknowledgements

•

i am beyond grateful to so many people in my life.
from strangers to my closest loved ones, i wouldn't be
here without every single one of you.

i would like to especially thank:
- mom & dad, for always supporting my writing
- my kuyas, for giving me new perspectives
- my little siblings, for making me laugh
- my best friend, a.h., for always being there
- k.d., for never giving up on me
- the nanowrimo community & its endless inspiration
- dr. canuso and ms. jackie, for helping me recover
- mrs. krull, for fostering my love for english and poetry
- mr. fazio, who saw potential in my poetry
- and Heavenly Father, for guiding me, even when i'm too stubborn to follow

www.ingramcontent.com/pod-product-compliance
Lightning Source LLC
Chambersburg PA
CBHW030855090426
42737CB00009B/1244